SUPERSTARS OF WRESTLING

BROCK LESNAR

BY BENJAMIN PROUDFIT

Gareth Stevens
PUBLISHING

HOT TOPICS

Please visit our website, www.garethstevens.com. For a free color catalog of all our high-quality books, call toll free 1-800-542-2595 or fax 1-877-542-2596.

Library of Congress Cataloging-in-Publication Data

Names: Proudfit, Benjamin, author.
Title: Brock Lesnar / Benjamin Proudfit.
Description: New York : Gareth Stevens Publishing, 2019. | Series: Superstars of wrestling | Includes index.
Identifiers: LCCN 2017045189| ISBN 9781538220955 (library bound) | ISBN 9781538220979 (pbk.) | ISBN 9781538220986 (6 pack)
Subjects: LCSH: Lesnar, Brock--Juvenile literature. | Wrestlers--United States--Biography--Juvenile literature.
Classification: LCC GV1196.L47 P76 2019 | DDC 796.812092 [B] --dc23 LC record available at https://lccn.loc.gov/2017045189

First Edition

Published in 2019 by
Gareth Stevens Publishing
111 East 14th Street, Suite 349
New York, NY 10003

Designer: Sarah Liddell
Editor: Kristen Nelson

Photo credits: Cover, pp. 1, 29 JP Yim/Stringer/Getty Images Entertainment/Getty Images; p. 5 Starship.paint/Wikimedia Commons; p. 7 Mark Mainz/Staff/Getty Images Entertainment/Getty Images; p. 9 NCAA Photos/Contributor/NCAA Photos/Getty Images; pp. 11, 27 Rey Del Rio/Stringer/Getty Images Sport/Getty Images; p. 13 Bill Greenblatt/Contributor/Getty Images Sport/Getty Images; p. 15 Theo Wargo/Staff/WireImage/Getty Images; p. 17 Tom Dahlin/Contributor/Getty Images Sport/Getty Images; p. 19 Icon Sports Wire/Contributor/Icon Sportswire/Getty Images; p. 21 Jon P. Kopaloff/Contributor/Getty Images Sport/Getty Images; p. 23 FlickrWarrior/Wikimedia Commons; p. 24 Frightwolf/Wikimedia Commons; p. 25 Shipjustgotreal/Wikimedia Commons.

Printed in the United States of America

CPSIA compliance information: Batch #CS18GS: For further information contact Gareth Stevens, New York, New York at 1-800-542-2595.

CONTENTS

THE FIGHTER

The "Beast **Incarnate**" Brock
Lesnar is big and strong
and would rather give an
opponent an F-5 than talk.
But he isn't just powerful
in the World Wrestling
Entertainment (WWE)
ring. Brock has been a very
successful amateur wrestler
and MMA fighter, too!

IN THE RING

Amateur wrestling is the form of wrestling most schools do. It takes place on a mat. MMA is mixed martial arts, a sport that combines many kinds of fighting sports.

5

EARLY LIFE

EARLY LIFE

Brock was born on July 12, 1977, in Webster, South Dakota. His parents were dairy farmers. Brock grew up helping on the farm. He told *Sports Illustrated*: "I knew if I could cut it on the farm, I could cut it anywhere."

IN THE RING

Today, Brock still loves to spend time outside hunting and fishing.

Brock wanted to get strong, so he worked really hard on the farm. His mom also started him in an amateur wrestling program at age 5—and she expected him to win. Brock was already learning to be a champion.

IN THE RING

Brock wrestled in the 98-pound (44 kg) class when he was in seventh grade!

9

WRESTLING SUCCESS

In high school, Brock started to get much bigger. He joined the National Guard at age 17, but didn't end up staying in long. Brock went to Bismarck Junior College in North Dakota and continued wrestling. He won the national heavyweight title in 1998.

IN THE RING

Brock was found to be red-green **color-blind**. That meant he couldn't get the job he wanted working with explosives in the National Guard!

After 2 years at junior college, Brock **transferred** to the University of Minnesota to wrestle. In 2000, he won the **NCAA** heavyweight championship! He left college with a record of 106 total wins and only 5 losses.

IN THE RING

In 1999, Brock had come in second at the NCAA championships.

13

TIME FOR PRO WRESTLING

Brock's success didn't go unnoticed. He was scouted by both the National Football League (NFL) and WWE, then called the World Wrestling Federation (WWF). He chose WWE! Brock started out in WWE's Ohio Valley Wrestling (OVW).

IN THE RING

Brock first appeared on WWE's TV show *Raw* in March 2002. Not long after, he became the WWE Champion! He was only 25, the youngest champion ever to hold that title at that time.

FOOTBALL NEXT

Brock was **dominating** in WWE, but he didn't like all the travel or the direction of his in-ring character. So, in 2004, he left to try out for the NFL. He went to the Minnesota Vikings training camp in July 2004, but didn't play on the team.

IN THE RING

In April 2004, Brock was in a bad motorcycle crash. This may have stopped him from playing his best at the Vikings camp.

17

IN THE RING OVERSEAS

In 2005, Brock decided to continue wrestling—just not for WWE. He went to Japan and wrestled for New Japan Pro Wrestling. He won the company's heavyweight title in his first match!

IN THE RING

In 2006, Brock married Rena, a WWE Diva whose in-ring name was Sable. They have two sons, Turk and Duke. Brock also has two other children named Luke and Mya.

RENA

19

THE UFC

Brock combined his in-ring **experience** and success in amateur wrestling to take on a new challenge in 2007: MMA. In February 2008, Brock lost his first **bout** in UFC (Ultimate Fighting Championship). But in November, he beat Randy Couture for the UFC title!

RANDY
COUTURE

IN THE RING

Brock **defended** the UFC Heavyweight Championship
at UFC 100 and UFC 116.

Brock lost the UFC title at UFC 121 on October 23, 2010. By then, he was having health problems that made fighting harder. He lost another bout in December 2011 and announced his **retirement** from UFC.

IN THE RING

Brock and his WWE in-ring manager Paul Heyman wrote a book together in 2011 called *Death Clutch: My Story of Determination, Domination, and Survival.*

PAUL
HEYMAN

23

BROCK'S BACK!

Brock spent some time getting healthy. Then, on April 2, 2012, the crowd went crazy as he showed up on *Raw* and gave superstar John Cena an F-5. After 8 years away from WWE, Brock was back!

JOHN CENA

IN THE RING

At WrestleMania 30, Brock broke the
winning streak of the Undertaker, who had never
lost a match at WrestleMania!

UFC 200

Brock dominated in WWE until 2016, when he wanted one more challenge. He came out of retirement for UFC 200 to fight Mark Hunt. The outcome of the bout was ruled "no contest," or a draw.

IN THE RING

Brock defeated Mark Hunt in UFC 200. Because he failed a drug test from before the bout, the outcome was changed to "no contest."

MARK
HUNT

27

THE UNIVERSAL CHAMP

In 2017, Brock took on Goldberg at WrestleMania 33 to win the WWE Universal title. Brock successfully defended the title in August at SummerSlam in a Fatal 4-Way match against Roman Reigns, Samoa Joe, and Braun Strowman. The "Beast" continues to conquer!

IN THE RING

Brock and his family live on a farm
in Saskatchewan, Canada.

THE BEST OF
BROCK LESNAR

SIGNATURE MOVES
spinebuster, belly-to-belly suplex, powerbomb

FINISHERS
F-5, kimura

ACCOMPLISHMENTS
NCAA wrestling champion; youngest WWE Champion ever at the time; WWE Universal Champion; UFC Heavyweight Champion; ended the Undertaker's WrestleMania winning streak

MATCHES TO WATCH
WrestleMania 31 vs. Roman Reigns, Extreme Rules 2012 vs. John Cena

BOUT TO WATCH
UFC 91 vs. Randy Couture

FOR MORE INFORMATION

BOOKS

Kortemeier, Todd. *Superstars of WWE*. Mankato, MN: Amicus High Interest, 2017.

Scheff, Matt. *Pro Wrestling's Greatest Rivalries*. Minneapolis, MN: SportsZone, 2017.

WEBSITES

Brock Lesnar
www.ufc.com/fighter/Brock-Lesnar?id=
Check out Brock Lesnar's official UFC stats.

Brock Lesnar
www.wwe.com/superstars/brock-lesnar
Visit Brock Lesnar's official WWE page.

GLOSSARY

bout: an athletic match

color-blind: unable to see the difference between some colors

defend: to stop someone from taking

dominate: to hold mastery over because of greater strength or skill

experience: having skills gained by doing something

incarnate: come to life in a human body

NCAA: National Collegiate Athletic Association

opponent: the person or team you must beat to win a game or match

retirement: the act of withdrawing from a type of work

transfer: to move from one place to another

INDEX